I0412451

THE COUPON MASTERY BOOK

ACT AND KEEP YOUR MONEY

BY MAXWELL D. TOLIVER

Volume III

THE COUPON MASTERY BOOK

The Coupon Mastery Book

Introduction:

In March of 2011, my wife and I decided to start couponing. We had looked at the coupon industry and this type of shopping twice before, but we never really came together as a family and agreed to use coupons.

Before it was either I wanted to do coupons and my wife did not or my wife would want to do the coupons but I did not. I think the other times it was about commitment to the time it takes. I think we really thought it would take more time then we wanted to give. The difference this time is that we both wanted to get involved. We had just brought our home and we wanted to maximize what our money could be doing for us.

The Toliver's

We have been living in what's called, "The favor of God" for more than about two years now. We focus on doing things according to God's word. So when we considered getting involved with couponing this time we were both concerned that we were doing the right thing according to God's word and also that we were managing our money correctly.

Now we know that many people may think that we are very religious and that this book will be more religion then it is about coupons. It's not! We just wanted everyone to understand where we are coming from. Because when you are living in God's favor you have to be careful about the things you get into and the things you do. The last thing we want to do is to step outside of God's favor. So getting involved with couponing was a big decision.

Couponing is really a way of life, a way of being and a type of mindset. Many people see it as being tight with our money or that couponing is only for people that are having money problems.

However, the reality is much different for us. You see, we try to be good stewards of our money. That means that we are very careful about how we make our money, how we spend, and how we invest our money. So once we were both on the same page, we were 'all in'.

Chapter 2: Learning Curve

I wanted to write this book, because I realized that as we were using coupons and people we were meeting were asking so many questions I wanted to be able to give answers that made sense. So, I promise that when you are done with this book and you are about four weeks into your coupons savings, you'll feel like you are ripping off the stores and that someone is going to come after you. It really does feel like you're doing something wrong at first. Then about two months after that you will feel angry when you have to pay full price for something.

Our learning curve was about 3 to 4 months. During that time we spent and saved about 50%. We had a hard time getting our savings to be higher than 50%, we kind of broke even. We were very unhappy and thought we were doing something very wrong. We could not put our fingers on it but we knew that something was really wrong.

Then, the TLC program came on TV in our area called, "Extreme Couponing." We recorded every show and sat down in front of the TV with pen and paper. We considered ourselves to be in school and truly we were. I am telling you we saw and found something's that changed the way we were using coupons. We would go over and over the recordings looking at the websites they showed and trying to find them online. We would try to understand some of the different tactics they were using to get all of the coupons they had. Then we focused on what the commentator was saying as he introduced the show and the people they were featuring. Then one day it all came together for us and we were off and running.

These days, we are saving on average about 70% or better. Often times, we can save up to 98% to 100%. That means that we pay only the taxes and sometimes we are paid to take the groceries out of the store. To put that in terms that makes sense, it means that for every $100 dollars in retail value we spend less than $30 and often the store pays us.

Look it is a real good feeling to come home with a bunch of food and still have the same amount of money in your pocket as when you left the house.

At the time of printing this book, we have saved over $3,000.00 and we have only been using coupons for 8 months. I don't know about some people's household but that is big for mine. Man, that's our electric bill for the year.

A short story;

One time we went to our local grocery store and brought $150.00 worth of products and when we finished with our coupons the store ended up giving us $10.00. Think about that! You can see some of our video shopping trips at **http://www.youtube.com/watch?v=mjupz69FwJQ&feature=share&list=PLE73A0516B36070BC**.

Another story;

We did a quick check online and found some real good deals so I hurried into CVS one day and every product I mean every product I was getting a lady was also getting. We made friends after the third product. I thought she was using coupons also, but she was not. She told me that she saw the sales in the newspaper and wanted the products.

I allowed her to check out first because I wanted to see what her total would be. The retail value of everything we both was $120.32. The store sale brought it down to $80.00. Which is what she paid and she got a CVS reward bucks of $20.00. She was happy.

But I was using coupons my cost for the same products was $35.00 and I also got a CVS rewards bucks of $20.00.

So it was like she paid $60.00, and it was like I paid $15.00 for $120 worth of products.

Chapter 3: Knowing What I Know

So my question is simple; do you want to know what I know?

Okay I guess you do…

Before we get into everything, I want to say this; I am going to tell you some things that no one has told us. I feel this is the best way to go about couponing. I discovered this one item too late and my wife and I believe it cost us greatly.

The very first thing is that this book is about grocery coupons, but I want you all to understand that there are coupons for almost everything you can think of and name.

Some facts:

Last year, there were 332 billion coupons issued and 3.3 billion redeemed.

There was $3.7 billion dollars' worth of coupons used in the United States.

You and I will come across hundreds of coupons that we will not use, and that will be thrown away.

Let's start:

I am going to start you off where I wish we had started. You'll be much happier with us and yourself. Okay so here are the big tips:

1. BEFORE you start getting any coupons at all get paper and a pen and go thought your pantry. List everything consumable in it. Why? Because these are the foods and toiletries you like to use often and would like to get more of these products before you get any other. Make sense?

2. Go online to each of their web sites and look for their coupon links and register to get their coupons or to get special marketing notices. We honestly wish we had of done this it would of saved us a ton of money.

3. Make sure you get your local store *'good customer cards.'* Get one for every adult (people over 16 or 18) in your household. This is very important to maximize your savings. Do not have your son sign up with you on your card. Everyone must have their own card not connected to each other. No matter what, the store rep says don't do it. Their job is to get people signed up on the plans. The store reps have no idea about the way coupons are handed out. The large stores have *'loyalty rewards'* and will monitor every user and sometimes the household in total. So if everyone has their own cards the store may send you some coupon gifts that will reflect your buying habits. *We have been*

around people who got their rewards at the same time we did and they get five coupons and we will get twenty coupons and we think it's because we have three cards attached to the house.

4. You need to get a separate email address that you use for just coupons. Nothing special needed just one devoted for coupons. You can go to http://www.hotmail.com for that. This way as you sign up to get your coupons they all go to one address. This is very important and you should do this ASAP. Trust me when I tell you, you will have hundreds of coupons coming to your email box in less than two weeks from now and they will not stop and you will have a hard time keeping up with them. It will feel like companies are just toughing coupons at you to use their products.

5. Another thing the gurus will not tell you about.....In most states there are coupons in the Wednesday newspapers called "RedPlum". It will never be mentioned in their trainings and on none of the coupon web sites I am going to tell you about acknowledge these coupons and there are quite a few coupons in this papers. So here is what you do to get the most out of your coupons. When you get extra coupons just cut all of the coupons out that you want and store them in you coupon book.

6. You will want to know what day of the week your local store starts their sales. That would be on Wednesday's for us here and the web sites post the coupons on Wednesday mornings. Those who are home when the coupons are posted get the deals early.

Would you like to know what inserts you need to look for each Sunday? This website will tell you that information and more.
http://**www.sundaycouponreview.com**

Chapter 4: You're System

Oh, yes, you need a system! Man, do you need a system. You need a place to store your coupons. We have used a least four different methods and we out grow them all except our current one so I'll tell you the two we use because they seem to work best.

1) We found something that looks like an old milk crate in Wal-Mart. We got some penda flex file holders (you need enough to hold about 30 files) they all fit into this crate well.

2) We have a 4" notebook. Don't get anything under a 3" book. If you can find one get a 5" book (It means that the rings are big) trust me you'll be happier. The book needs pockets and the more the better.

3) You need "Baseball Card Holders," and Wal-Mart sells these but the best place to get the better quality is the comic book stores. If you tell them you are a coupon person they will give you what you need. The best holders are the ones that hold 4 to 6 slots of baseball cards. You will also need separator labels like you're in school for each subject. But you want the alphabet ones.

4) You may want to get the old flexible pencil holders the children use (one for each store you like to

visit) and put the coupons you intended on using that day in the holders.

For more beginners' tips, you can go to http://**www.grocerypricebooks.com**

The coupons that come in the Sunday paper you put into the file holders and the coupons you print out you put into your book.

Another rule…whenever you go shopping you always take your book(s) with you, every time! As you build up your coupons you will understand why. If there is a sale in the store that your websites have missed you may have coupons for the item on sale and you'll be glad again.

FACT: Prices change frequently. For many coupons users the sale price is the only price they're willing to pay.

Another story: This just happened yesterday. *Back ground*…we have been getting 2 liters of soda for about ohhhh FREE to about $.25 for months. We were in CVS and the soda I wanted was only $.78 and I asked my wife if I could get it LOL. I asked for a reason because I knew the answer. She said, "we have twelve 2 liters at home that we have paid nothing for.

15

Why do you want to pay anything for this one little soda?" That is the mindset you'll be getting soon.

Chapter 5: How many coupons do you need

A) Well, this of course is up to you. The more coupons you have the more products you can get.

We have never heard a 'rule of thumb' so I say two more coupons then the number of people in your house hold. So I will use my household to help with some numbers. I have 4 and a half people. My grandson is 4 years old. So we like to get 6 to 8 coupons per product each week.

I know, WOW, you say? Not really, we really need to get 10 coupons per item to have a good supply. If you think about it we all eat and use products. In my house a box of spaghetti can be eaten in one night. So having 6 to 8 boxes at a time is only a week's worth of spaghetti. So we have not really done anything special unless we get the 8 boxes and eight bottles of spaghetti sauce for $2.00 or less. Then we did something.

How can you get products for FREE?

This is how it happens so you can relax about this issue. The product normally is sold for $4.00 per item. The store has a sale for 'buy 10 for $10" that means that each product is on sale for only $1.00 each. You have coupons that read $.50 off of one of the same product. But your store rounds every manufactures coupon up to $1.00. So that product is FREE for you. And if you have 8 coupons for that item then you get all 8 items for FREE.

Where do we get our major supply?

B) The best place by far is your areas newspaper. We pay for six newspapers to come to our household every Sunday. Okay, really we get a newspaper five days a week but Sunday is the big day. There are the store sales which come on different days so we need them to plan our trips.

C) Once you get your coupons from the Sunday paper, you will need to label them all. There are two systems we us and so will you so here is the best way to label your coupons. Make sure there are no coupons you want on the front inside cover of the book and use permanent black ink "Sharpie." On each book, write the date they were in the Sunday's paper and you will list the codes (couponsense) gives you each week. This way no matter what web site you are on you can find the coupons you need, because some sites use the date system and 'couponsense' uses the code system.

Minor coupons:

D) We call these minor coupons because they are coupons that we have to go after. These are the *Electronic Store Coupons*. You go to the web sites and pick the products you want to add to your store card. These coupons do not print out they are added to your card. But you may print out your savings list so you do know what is on your card.

E) Next are the coupons that you print out. Warning...this is not a joke. You need a good printer, but pay attention to how much the ink costs to replace it. Also important is how many color and black & white copies you can get before you need to replace the ink. The machine will tell you how many copies you can get. But you will need to ask about the cost per ink cartridges.

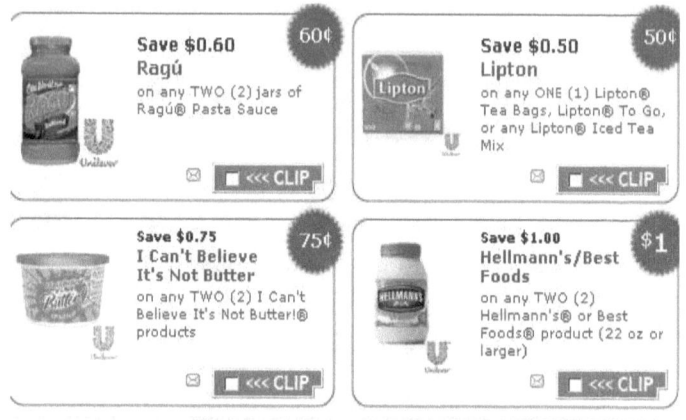

Save $0.60 — 60¢
Ragú
on any TWO (2) jars of Ragú® Pasta Sauce
⊠ ■ ‹‹‹ CLIP

Save $0.50 — 50¢
Lipton
on any ONE (1) Lipton® Tea Bags, Lipton® To Go, or any Lipton® Iced Tea Mix
⊠ ■ ‹‹‹ CLIP

Save $0.75 — 75¢
I Can't Believe It's Not Butter
on any TWO (2) I Can't Believe It's Not Butter!® products
⊠ ■ ‹‹‹ CLIP

Save $1.00 — $1
Hellmann's/Best Foods
on any TWO (2) Hellmann's® or Best Foods® product (22 oz or larger)
⊠ ■ ‹‹‹ CLIP

Now why is this so important? Because once you start finding the coupons you want you'll be printing like crazy. So you will also want to know all the above information. I go through a ream of paper (500 sheets) and ink every month and a half without fail. So this is the expensive part of couponing. But if you want the deals you got to print the coupons.

Note: Coupons you have to print are from the manufactures and they only release a certain amount of them and when they are gone they are simply gone.

Now you should know that you can only print out each coupon two times from each computer and yes they can tell how many times you have printed that one coupon. So the best thing to do is to have more dedicated computers you use for printing coupons. So if you have a lap top and a desk top I would use them both on coupon printing days.

Chapter 6: Coupon Terms

If you have seen the TV show, then you might be familiar with some of the terms, but in case you are not here are some of the most popular terms.

- ALL YOU - ALL YOU MAGAZINE (MFG. COUPON)
- BOGO or B1G1 - BUY ONE GET ONE (FREE)
- B&M - BRICK AND MORTAR (PHYSICAL STORES LOCATIONS)
- CRT - CASH REGISTER TAPE
- DND - DO NOT DOUBLE (COUPON)
- ECB or ECBs - EXTRA CARE BUCKS (CVS)
- GM - GENERAL MILLS COUPON INSERT (inside Sunday paper)
- MFG or MFR - MANUFACTURER
- MIR - MAIL IN REBATE
- MM - MONEYMAKER
- OOP - OUT OF POCKET (CASH PAID)
- OYNO or OYNP - ON YOUR NEXT ORDER or ON YOUR NEXT PURCHASE
- PEELIE - ON PACKAGE COUPON
- PG or P&G - PROCTER AND GAMBLE COUPON INSERT (Inside Sunday paper)

- PRINTABLE - PRINTABLE COUPON
- PSA - PRICES STARTING AT
- RP - REDPLUM COUPON INSERT (inside Sunday paper)
- RR or RRs - REGISTER REWARDS (WALGREENS)
- SS - SMART SOURCE COUPON INSERT (Inside Sunday paper)
- STACK - USE A STORE COUPON AND A MFG. COUPON ON A SINGLE ITEM
- YMMV - YOUR MARKET MAY VARY
- VV - VIDEO VALUE (RITE AID STORE COUPONS)
- W-IVC - WALGREENS INSTANT VALUE COUPONS (WAGS STORE COUPON)
- WYB - WHEN YOU BUY

Okay, there are some things I want to tell you all about. You have heard the term, "Dumpster Diving," when people go to extreme measures and go to garbage dumps and go looking for coupons. To me these are the same kinds of people that would get addicted to drugs, alcohol or any other thing that is addictive.

The only thing I will do is at the self-check outs in the store they have a garbage box because people tend to want to throw away these things called "Catalina".   They are making a big mistake. I take what they get rid of and save $3 to $5 on my next shopping trip.

Above you have the list of coupons that come in the Sunday paper. Now I will give you all of the web sites we use to get coupons. Some of the web sites use the same coupon vendor so you'll have to go through them all.

The last thing I want to talk to you about is that there are two types of coupon sites. There are the national coupons bloggers and the local bloggers. If you live outside of AZ, where I live, some of the local web sites may not work for you. The way around this is to go to google.com and type in "coupons online" and what is available in your area should come up along with the national web site.

Many of these web sites are run by individual people who will also teach you even more about couponing than what I have in this short book.

Chapter 7: Web Sites

My disclaimer about these web sites; these people are well just that, people and they make mistakes and none of these web sites catch all of the sales and the coupons that go along with them. That is why we have learned to use three or four sites at all times. Below are our top four web sites that we use all the time.

Let's start with one that you have to pay to get into but it is worth it. This is our main web site, because we are able to keep track of our spending.

http://www.couponsense.com before you venture to this site call, Andrea VanHorn at 623-825-9772 and she will give you a password. The cost for this web site is $15 a month. She will also ask you, "Who referred you?" Tell her that "Janice Toliver" did. She will have a few other questions for you.

So why pay for any site? This one we pay for because it is a good, simple site for what you will need. She has a forum on the site where people talk about their daily shopping trips and they tell you what coupons they used, where to find them and even what combination to use them in to get the best deals. There are training videos available and one of the most important things that we like is that you can keep track of the money you have spent for every single shopping trip for the entire year. So you know what you have spent, what you have saved and the amount of coupons you have used. That's how I know how much we have saved from when we started. Another good feature that all the sites give you is that they email you twice a week with updates and when new coupons are available. I use this site almost every day for one thing –

"Freebies" baby. Oh, yes, there is FREE stuff all the time, every day all over the place. Some you have to go to in your car and many you just have to go online and follow the instructions. I have gotten Ice Cream, Lotion, Candy, Chicken, Shaving stuff, and more. It's cool to check it out in the morning and when I have a business meeting I always schedule the meeting around or near the free offer for the day. I normally meet with one person at a time so if the deal fits the person I am meeting I'll print out a coupon for the both of us and treat them. They get a kick out of getting something for free and wonder how I did it all the time. It keeps the conversation going and lightens up the mood sometimes and oh yes I get a tax write off the entire full price of the item.

Another story:

One day, I met with a man that needed some work done on his web site. I knew where he lived and worked. It just happened that there was a company listed on the web site that was holding a barbeque to bring in more customers. I scheduled the meeting to be next door and just before the time stated. Of course I made sure that we were able to take a break and I treated him to a full lunch on that company. He was excited and I got the job with ease.

All of the rest of the websites are FREE:

http://www.coupondivas.com

(real good training and information), this site is good because she give you very specific training for certain stores. She tells some secrets of the trade that will save you a ton of money as soon as you walk into the door. She has over 100 videos that will make you an expert in the store of your choice.

http://www.couponmom.com

This website helps with knowing the value of the sales, and this is something that I can't stress enough how important it is to know.

Here is why… Your favorite hot dogs are on sale in two stores. The price is close enough that you would buy them at which ever store you happen to be at. But if you were on this site you would have found out that neither price is really good because they hiked up the price from its normal price a few weeks ago. So the savings is only 60%

if you were to purchase it this week. Whereas if you were to hold off maybe and waited two or three weeks the hot dogs will be on big time sale from their hiked up price (happens more often than you think) and now the sale price is so low and you happen to have that same coupon available that it makes the cost almost free. I have gotten a pack of hotdogs at $0.25 each.

http://www.thekrazycouponlady.com

This is good training and information when you are setting up your system you'll need to make a "Coupon Book". This web site tells you the two most popular ways people make their books. She also gives good training and coupons to be printed and put on your store cards.

Chapter 8: Getting more coupons

Well there are millions of coupons to get and many don't get claimed. You'll see as the months pass by you'll be throwing out those that have expired and replacing them with newer coupons.

But you can also load coupons onto your store cards and your smart phone. Below are lists of web sites that allow you to do either one or both Medias.

http://www.ppgazette.com

http://www.shortcuts.com/stores

http://www.redplum.com – comes in your newspaper and you can get more coupons online.

http://www.smartsource.com – Also come in your newspaper and there are more coupons available online.

http://www.afullcup.com

http://www.pgeverydaysolutions.com – also come in your Sunday newspaper and there are more coupons online.

http://www.greengiant.com

http://www.savingstar.com

http://www.lactaid.com – Not everyone can drink whole milk. So here you go guys.

http://www.livingrichwithcoupons.com

http://www.shopathome.com

The only magazine we found that have real good coupons is www.allyou.com this is also a magazine that you must get. They have a lot of coupons in it often times over $60 worth.

Chapter 9: Extra Coupons

You will not believe this but how about getting some extra coupons? That would be good right? Well, how about hundreds of extra coupons on demand, now that would be real good! Here are some web sites where you can by extra coupons.

http://www.amazon.com and search for "coupons"

Now these websites have people working for them and they have a whole lot of coupons. You can get 50 coupons for one product if you want.

BIG SECRET HERE:

Okay, this is a 'how they do that' kind of secret. If you have seen the TV show you have seen the people almost clean the store out it seems right? Well here is how that happens.

In my area the store sales start on Wednesdays at 12am. All of the web sites post there finds at around 12 pm Wednesday. But those who want to take maximum advantage of the sales do two things. They may show up at 5 or 6am on Wednesday morning and walk the isles and they are waiting on their computers for the postings.

Now with the information they have from their walk through and the information they get online about what sales are found and the coupons available, they will pick the ones they want that are hot deals (the FREE stuff and almost free stuff) from +$0.01 (this is better worded as the store ends up paying you money to take the item out of the store. The highest I have seen this is +$50.00) to about $0.30 a peace for each item.

Once they have the items they want, they contact these web sites below and request a bunch of the coupons. So back to hot dogs… the Favorite Hot Dog Company has their dogs on sale for $.70 a pack. The available coupon from three weeks ago is for $.50 off a pack but your store doubles every coupon up to $1.00 right now. Well that makes every pack of Favorite Hot Dogs FREE. So they order 50 coupons from the bulk coupon site below and that may cost them $5.00 or less! They are told what date the coupons will arrive at their house, let's say Friday. Now they get on the phone at about 1pm and call the store with the sale and place a large order for Saturday at 5pm to pick up their Favorite Hot Dogs. When they pick them up it is still within the sales period and they hand in their 50 coupons and all fifty packs of hot dogs are FREE. They may have to do many check outs but who cares. They got the entire thing for $5.00 total out of pocket. It would have cost them $35 for all 50 packs of the Favorite Hot Dogs.

So here are these all important sites.

http://www.thecouponclippers.com

http://www.couponsthingsbydede.com

http://www.manufacturerscoupons.net

http://www.thecouponmaster.com

I told you there are coupons for almost everything right? Well, here you go....but if you are really seeking coupons for certain things I suggest you goggle it.

http://www.shopathome.com

http://www.restaurant.com

http://www.freebiefindingmom.com

I told you about those "Catalina" coupons right? Well, here is the web site

http://www.couponnetwork.com

I love this site because here are the products that really count. This site offers you discounts on product that you buy in bulk, real cool.

Below are some web sites for some stores. But there are coupons for almost every store you can think of. You should learn the coupon policies of each store because they are very different. The top four web sites will give you even more stores that have coupons and they will even tell you what coupons are good at the store you want to use this week.

Coupons can be used almost anywhere, even Wal-Mart. They claim to have the lowest prices and will match any other store that has a lower price, right? Well, how about matching the prices and then add a coupon on top of that low price. We do it all the time and remember we are not just talking about food and beauty items.

http://www.walmart.com

http://www.safeway.com

http://www.jcpenney.com

http://www.frysfood.com

Chapter 10: Discount Thinking

After you have gone a while in doing coupons I guess you start to think about the things you don't know about. What am I missing? Well I have a few things we have discovered sense I first wrote this book and I'll add them here.

The first topic is your Birthday. This is an assume topic because it is all about you and no one else, unless you are a twin or there are just more of well you. But here is the deal.

I wanted to take my wife out for her birthday to one of the many nice restaurants in our area.

I did not want to come across cheap in anyway but I did want to surprise her with how smart I am, LOL.

So I went online about a month before her birthday and picked a place that I knew she would like. I filled out the information to be notified about specials they would have but I used both of our names and birthdays.

Three days before her birthday she gets a text on her phone giving her a discount on her meal if she comes in on her birthday and eats in the restaurant. You know the light bold went on and I applied to a few more places we liked and on our birthdays we get offers to eat at a discount in all the places I applied to.

I also did the same thing with a few jewelry stores in the area and the same thing happened.

So the lesion I learned is that customer service is not dead at all. You just have to tell the store you are a valued customer and they will offer you a discount to keep you happy.

The second topic I wanted to address is Store Loyalty Cards: I know I have covered this already but I wanted to talk about a different aspect of using them. Here is my story and why it became noteworthy.

About a week ago I needed to make some copies of a flyer for my upcoming workshops "Get Your Financial Breakthrough In 2013" and attend "OH GOD! What's Going on with My Money" which you can learn more about at http://www.nomorew4s.com

I went to my local Staples and when I went to check out the girl behind the counter told me that they were running a sale today and that I would get a discount on the copies. Then she asked me if I had a store discount card and I said no. She asked me if I would like one. I said yes just because I did not have one and I figured I would use it often in 2013. So she added my wife and I to the store discount list and we got an extra 10% off our purchase.

That example got me thinking a little bit. Then the other day there was a TV show commercial that got my attention. The store offered a sale on their suites and then a one day special which was buy one suite and get three free. A few days later it hit me and I got mad at myself because I did not take advantage of the sale. But here is what I came up with: If they already have a sale going on and they are also offering a one day mage sale it would be outstanding if I were to go to the store and ask for a store discount card on top of the two sales. WOW I thought a serious discount would be available to the person that understood how to work discounts.

I did contact the store to make sure what I was thinking would have worked and they said, yes. So I think it is worth mentioning that we should get store discount cards but maybe time when you want to get each stores card because you can get some really good deals from stores that offer a card and an instant discount when you sign up.

The third topic I which to talk about is Wal-Mart ad matching: Now this is a story that I wanted to share because it got me excited and I intend on looking at it again this Sunday.

My wife discovered this by accident believe it or not. Now granted many of you may already know about this but we are not big Wal-Mart fans. Therefore this was a discovery for us.

Now this store has a saying that they will match or beat their competitors. And they often have ads about their ad-matching program. Well this is just another type of discount program with its own rules.

My wife decided to go shopping and she wanted to go to Wal-Mart to ad-match some fruit and vegetables which she does often. But this time she saw an ad in the paper from another store that offered a sale on Top Round Roast for $7 and she said she would try to ad-match it but was not sure if Wal-Mart did that for meat. Well they do and the $13.49 Roast cost us only $7 then we found out that they do it for all their products. So check with the ads from other stores for clothing and electronic and everything before you go to Wal-Mart. You just might find some real good deals.

The last new topic I wanted to talk about is also pretty well known but there are still people who don't understand or think they are too good for coupons or something so I wanted to bring this topic up.

I am sure that you have heard of the "Entertainment Book"! You can get it almost anywhere but you can also go to http://www.entertainmant.com. This is a real powerful book because it has hundreds of coupons in it from all of the stores you and I use the most. The coupons are often really good discounts as well.

For those who think it is not so good a deal at about $20 per book think of it this way. If I took my family of 5 out to eat just to McD's and we all get a sandwich, fries and a drink it would cost me between $30 and $35 dollars. But if I had the entertainment book it may just cost me about $20 depending on what everyone orders. We get two books every year because the deals are that good and we don't want to run out of the coupons.

Chapter 11: Money Saving Ideas

There are many things we spend money on that we really don't need. We pay more for utilities than we should; we buy things we don't have a real need for; and we literally waste money that could be put to better use if we spent a little more time keeping track of where our money goes.

To help those who are reading my book I've compiled a huge list of effective ways to save money and help you stick to your family budget.

1. Avoid Overage Charges on Cell phones (Savings $10-$200/month)

If you find you are paying extra every month for consistently using more minutes than your plan allows, or sending or receiving more texts than your plan allows – it may be less expensive to switch to a plan with a bigger allowance for minutes and texts each month.

"I once was hit with a $200 charge for going over minutes and texts!" – Jon

2. Weatherize Your Home (Savings: 25-40% of heating and cooling expenses)

If you weatherize your home, you'll help keep hot air in during the winter and help keep your home cooler during the hotter months. It has been shown that when air leaks are plugged and sealed in a home, you can save between 25-40% on heating and cooling bills.

Homeowners may receive the most benefit for the least expense and effort by weatherizing their home, compared to many other types of home improvements. Even a home that has been well-insulated can lose up to 30% of its heat through cracks around windows and doors. Start by applying weather stripping to all of your windows and doors. If you'd like to try more advanced methods of weatherizing your home to further reduce your heat or cooled air loss, try this list of <u>weatherization tips</u>.

3. Quit smoking (Savings: High)

With the cost of a pack of cigarettes ranging from $4.74 (West Virginia) to $11.90 (New York), you can save a lot of money if you quit smoking. At half a pack per day, you would save between $16.59 to $41.65 per week (depending on where you live). Plus, smoking is bad for your health.

4. Re-Evaluate Cell Phone Plans and Data Plans at Least Once a Year (Savings $30 – $40 / Month)

If you are currently paying for an unlimited plan, but find you consistently use less phone minutes than one of the limited monthly plans your provider offers, or you don't send or receive more texts than one of the limited monthly plans allows – you could be spending more than you need. Always make sure you are using the correct plan for your typical usage.

Jon saved money on his cell phone plan this year: "I saved $30 a month as of January 2012 by updating my old phone and internet plan. That is going to save me $360 a year!"

Debbie saved money on her cell phone plan last year: "I was paying for an unlimited text and minute plan, but found I never went over 400 minutes per month. I kept the unlimited texts and dropped my talk minutes down to 450 per month, saving $20 per month."

5. Pay Off Credit Cards (Savings: High)

Credit card interest rates eat away at your money, month after month. Paying off your high-interest credit cards is one of the best investments you can make. Use the Debt Reduction Calculator to see how quickly you can pay off your debts.

6. Pay Off Credit Cards in Full Each Month (Savings: Moderate)

You can save money by avoiding future interest on credit card purchases. Make it a policy to never use credit cards to spend money you don't have. Keep track of every purchase made on your card, just as you would with a checking account, and pay off your card in full each month. If you can't maintain that type of discipline, tear up your cards.

7. Eat Out Less (Savings: High)

If you eat in restaurants or grab take-out twice a week for an average of $80 a week, you can put money back in your pocket simply by making all of your own meals. The typical cost for a chicken parmesan dinner at an average restaurant is about $15 – you can make the same meal (and healthier) for under $5 at home.

8. Downsize Your Home or Apartment (Savings: $200+ per month)

Moving into a smaller home or finding a cheaper apartment could significantly reduce your mortgage or rent payment. The average 3-bedroom apartment in rural New York rents for around $950 a month – downsize to a 2-bedroom apartment in the same area and you would pay an average of $700 a month rent. Consider this approach if you are needing to make very large long-term budget cuts.

9. Refinance when it makes Sense
(Savings: High)

You can save hundreds of dollars a month refinancing your mortgage, if the conditions are right. For example, if you have a mortgage with a $100,000 balance remaining, and you pay $1,250 per month with an interest rate of 7% – refinancing the balance with a 5% interest rate would save you $665.41 per month on your mortgage payment!

This assumes you don't lengthen or shorten your mortgage repayment term. Use a <u>mortgage calculator</u> to help you figure out your savings when you refinance.

*Note: Make sure you see what fees are involved in refinancing your mortgage, and calculate your savings after you account for refinancing costs in the form of attorney fees, application fees, inspections and any other fees.

10. Refill Bottled Water with Filtered Water (Savings: $38 per month or more)

Seriously? Yes. Instead of buying a 20-oz bottle of water each day for an average of $1.29 per bottle, you could refill your bottle with filtered water from the tap or fridge and save over $38 a month on just one bottle per day. Buy a water filter (Brita makes an on-the-go filtered water bottle for a one-time cost of $8.99 and filters 40 gallons before it needs replacing) and refill your bottle all day long for free.

11. Drink Water Instead of Soda
(Savings: $22-$67 per month)

If you drink an average of 3 cans of soda per day, you spend an average of $22.50 (based on buying twelve-packs of soda and an average price of $3 per pack). If you buy your soda from a vending machine for $.75 each, you're spending around $67 a month on soda! Switch to water and drink for free. Water is also healthier!

12. Buy Groceries in Bulk (Savings: Moderate)

When groceries and paper products are on sale, it makes sense to buy in bulk according to a 3-month storage plan. Keep three months' worth of these items stored in your home and you will only need to re-stock when the items are on sale again. You'll always get the best prices and never run out.

13. Keep Track of Ideal Prices on a Master Grocery List (Savings: Moderate)

Many items regularly go on sale at your favorite grocery stores. If you keep track of the prices and time of month or year when the items are on sale, you will know when to buy each of the items to get the best prices on them. You can also refer to your ideal price list when shopping in other stores to see if you are getting a good deal or not. Try one of Vertex42's grocery lists for keeping track of your frequently purchased items.

14. Avoid Impulse Buys (Savings: Moderate)

Create a shopping list and stick to it. If your grocery list includes items in your 3-month storage plan, buy them only if they happen to be on sale. Making a list ensures that get what you need and reduces the number of trips to the store. It also helps prevent buying an item just because it catches your eye. Never go to the store hungry.

15. Don't Pay for Unneeded Features (Savings: Moderate)

Salespeople are good at their jobs. Before making large purchases, do your research before going to the store. Arm yourself with information, sample prices, and deals offered by other stores. Decide ahead of time exactly what features you need and want, and don't let the sales person convince you to tack on another $100 for that extra feature you don't really need.

16. Avoid Paying for Extended Warranties (Savings: Moderate)

There is big money to be made these days selling extended warranties to naive consumers. Extended warranties are even being offered on low-cost items. Usually, store warranties are offered at the last minute as you are checking out, so you have very little time to think about or research the offer. There ARE times when you may need to use a warranty, but lemons usually show themselves during the first year and would be covered under the manufacturer's warranty. According to Consumer Reports (July 2011), "most repairs do not occur during the limited time period covered by the extended warranty."

One policy that works quite well is this: Don't purchase a warranty for an item that you can easily do without or can easily afford to replace. For all others, and especially for high-price items, do your research before you go to the checkout.

17. Choose Cheaper Dining Options
(Savings: Moderate)

If you can't eliminate take-out or eating in restaurants completely, learn to make less expensive menu selections. Order water instead of soda or alcoholic beverages and save $2 to $6 per meal. Choose a meal that will provide you with enough leftovers for another meal, and you'll stretch your dining budget further. Avoid ordering dessert. Have some ice cream when you get home, instead – it will be a lot cheaper, and you'll likely forget about the dessert anyway. Here are an additional 5 tips for saving money when eating in restaurants from Wisebread.com.

18. Cancel Cable/Satellite TV
(Savings: $50 to $150 a month)

Cable and satellite television programming is getting increasingly expensive. It's not uncommon for families to spend $150 a month to watch TV. You can put most of that money back into your family budget by using Netflix, Boxee or a Roku internet TV box to stream television shows and movies to your TV instead of cable or satellite service.

19. Pack a Lunch instead of Eating Out (Savings: $35 per week, $140 per month)

Do you usually buy lunch on work days? Spending just $7 a day on lunch, 5 days a week adds $35 a week to your food expenses. Bring last night's dinner leftovers or other packed lunch from home daily and save $35 a week, or an average of $140 a month. Our meal planner helps you plan ahead to ensure you have everything you need to pack a lunch and avoid the last minute take-out when you aren't sure what to make!

20. Avoid the Vending Machine (Savings: $6.25 a week, $25 per month)

With the average vending machine snack costing $1.25, you can save over $6.25 a week if you stopped buying one snack per day. Quickly deposit your small bills and change into the bank or keep it at home to help avoid the vending machine temptation.

21. Work Out at Home (Savings: $30-80 per month)

It is possible to get a good workout from home. If you learn to incorporate fitness without the gym membership, you can save between $30 and $80 per month (depending on your current gym membership costs). You could try using Vertex42's daily exercise log or weekly workout chart to help you reach your health and fitness goals on a budget.

22. Keep Track of Cash (Savings: Moderate)

Cash is easily spent, and most of us don't keep track of where our cash goes the way we do purchases made by check or debit card. Write down every penny you spend for a period of two weeks or more, and see where you are wasting cash. You can use the information learned from this process to develop a monthly budget.

When I kept track of my expenses for one month, it was quite the eye opening experiment. We had video rental late fees, and a lot more money was spent on take-out meals and convenience store trips than expected! In a month's time, we had spent over $210 on things we didn't plan for.

23. Don't Covet (Savings: Moderate)

Sheryl Crow says it best in the lyrics of a song: "It's not having what you want; it's wanting what you've got". If you learn to accept what you have and not covet the things you don't have – you'll save considerable amounts of money each year.

24. Make Less Expensive Friends (Savings: Moderate)

If you have many friends who only want to dine in expensive restaurants or seek out high-cost activities for entertainment, it may be time to make some new, less expensive friends. We don't mean to be callous, just realistic.

25. Choose a Car with Good Gas Mileage (Savings: Moderate)

When buying a car, pick a car that offers the best gas mileage for the most affordable price to get the best savings when commuting to and from work every day. If you're not sure what mileage your car is getting, use Vertex42's gas mileage log to help you figure it out.

26. Avoid Automotive Service Contracts (Savings: $200-$500)

So, you're about to finalize the purchase of a car and the dealer begins talking to you about what a great deal their service contract is. Just say no. Instead, follow the advice offered by Consumer Reports (July 2011) and stick the money into your savings to budget for future repairs and the recommended maintenance schedule.

"Avoiding the service contract also gives you the freedom to get your oil changed at cheaper (and faster) service stations." – Jon

27. Use Public Transportation (Savings: Moderate)

If you live in an area where it makes sense to use public transportation, you can avoid buying a car, avoid paying car insurance, and avoid paying for gas each week.

28. Carpool (Savings: Moderate)

Share commuting costs with others and you can reduce your travel expenses considerably. Find another traveler or two and take turns driving each other to and from work each week.

29. Don't Get a Pet (Savings: Moderate)

If you're looking to keep to a strict budget, reconsider getting a pet. Between veterinarian bills, supplies and pet food – having a pet can get expensive.

30. Garden (Savings: Low to Moderate)

Instead of buying all of your fruits, vegetables and herbs, consider an in-season garden. Your savings will depend on how much you normally buy of these produce items that you can grow on your own, but it can really add up. Some vegetables and herbs can be frozen, too – which helps you keep more of your home grown produce available even when the garden season ends.

31. Use Farmers Markets and/or Co-Ops (Savings: Low to Moderate)

Buy produce you can't grow yourself from a farmers market or through a <u>food co-op</u>. Buying from a farmers market or co-op often allows you to buy produce in bulk for less than you pay in the store.

32. Become Friends with the Library (Savings: Moderate)

Instead of buying or renting books, movies and music, start using your local library. Many libraries are even equipped to lend ebooks for your e-readers.

33. Challenge Property Tax Assessment (Savings: Moderate to High)

If your home seems to be assessed too high, you can challenge the assessment. If you are awarded with an adjustment, you could save a few hundred dollars or more per year on your property taxes.

34. Plan Vacations Far in Advance (Savings: Moderate)

Sometimes you can get great last minute deals, but when you plan a vacation in advance you can research your options and choose the one that gives you the most bang for your buck. You also have more time to budget the costs and are less likely to rely on credit cards to go on vacation.

35. Budget for Home and Car Maintenance (Savings: Moderate)

What do people do if their roof needs to be repaired or their car breaks down unexpectedly if they don't have money saved? They finance the repairs with a credit card or loan – and pay more than the total cost of maintenance because of interest. Experts calculate home maintenance costs at about 2% of your home's value each year, so open a bank account and make sure you set aside enough to cover your maintenance expenses. To keep track of how much money you have saved toward each of your savings goals, you can use Vertex42's savings goal tracking spreadsheet.

36. Shop at Thrift Stores (Savings: Moderate)

You can get jeans with the tags still on them for $2 at a thrift store! Before hitting the mall when you need clothes, try the thrift store. You might be surprised at what you can find, and at substantial savings.

37. Eliminate Bank Fees (Savings: $5-$20 / month)

Make sure you're not paying checking account maintenance fees, atm fees, credit card annual fees, or late fees. If you are, make changes to your bank and credit card company. Sign up for automatic payments on anything you have paid late in the past to make sure you don't miss a payment.

38. Use Coupons Only When it Makes Sense (Savings: Low to Moderate)

Don't buy items just because you have a coupon for them! Match coupons to items you will buy anyway and preferably when the item is on sale to increase your savings even more. If the sale and/or coupon price of an item is still higher than the generic version – buy the generic.

I regularly use coupons combined with my store's "buy one, get one free" deals. I like to watch for coupons that are for products already on sale. My favorite are the buy one get one free sales combined with coupons. I stock up on items like laundry detergent, dish soap, and freezer items and get two for less than the price of one!

39. Conserve Electricity (Savings: Low to Moderate)

Many of your appliances and electronics pull electricity even when they're not being used, and even if they are turned off. If you leave chargers plugged into the wall, they will use some electricity (even if they're not attached to anything). Phantom electricity adds up, and it's a waste of money.

Unplug everything that doesn't need to run unless you are using power strips – when not in use, you can hit the off switch on the power switch and cut the power supply off to everything plugged into that power strip. There are some appliances this won't work for – you wouldn't want to plug your refrigerator into a power strip to turn off, for example!

But for just about everything else – the toaster, coffee maker, microwave, televisions, radios, computers, and electronic games, only plug them in when you're using them and you'll start to see savings on your electric bill over time.

Other ways to reduce electricity costs is to switch out your light bulbs with the lower energy versions and turn lights off when they're not needed instead of leaving every light in the house blazing all night long. Here are 13 other ways to save money on electricity from SmartMoney.com.

40. Use a Clothes Line (Savings: $127 per year)

Instead of running the dryer for every load of laundry, get a clothes line and let them air dry. The average cost per load of laundry is $.35 cents (with an electric dryer) and the average American family dries 365 loads per year for a total of $127.75 a year.

41. Conserve Water (Savings: Low)

If your water is metered and you pay based on the amount of water you use, learning to conserve water will lower your water bill. The less water you use, the less you'll spend and water conservation has the added benefit of being better for the environment. Fill a plastic water or soda bottle with a few pebbles or sand and water; and place it into the toilet tank. Most toilets will flush just as well with a water bottle submerged in the tank, and will save about half a gallon to a gallon per flush.

Need some other ways to conserve water in your home? Here are 100 ways to conserve water from WaterUseItWisely.com.

42. Buy Generic Brands (Savings: 25 – 50%)

When grocery shopping and buying medications, consider buying generic instead of brand names to save money. For example, when buying aspirin, the generic brand is required by the Food and Drug Administration to be just as effective as the brand name aspirin, but is often sold for half the price of the brand name version.

Little Steps: 100 Great Tips For Saving Money For Those Just Getting Started

What follows is **a list of 100 more steps to take.** Each of these tactics are simple little moves you can make to improve your financial situation. Some of them take just a few minutes, others might take an hour or two, some of them require a bit of regular effort, but they're all incredibly simple – anyone can do them. Each of them also save significant money, especially over the long haul, and when combined together these tips can save you a lot of money *now*.

Obviously, **not all of these tips will apply to everyone.** Just go through the list and find ten or fifteen that *do* apply to you and use them in your life – you'll quickly find yourself saving some serious scratch.

1. Switch your bank accounts to a bank that respects you. You shouldn't be spending your hard-earned money on maintenance fees – you also should be earning some serious interest on your checking and savings accounts. I use ING Direct as my primary bank – I earn roughly 3% on my checking account and 3.4% on my savings account and they've never dinged me with a fee. Here's a guide on how to make that switch.

2. Turn off the television. One big way to save money is to watch less television. There are a lot of financial benefits to this: less exposure to guilt-inducing ads, more time to focus on other things in life, less electrical use, and so on. It's great to unwind in the evening, but seek another hobby to do that.

3. Turn a critical eye to your "collections." Most people collect something – what do you collect? Is it something that consistently brings you joy? Or is it something that you just do out of habit at this point? Does the collection itself have value? Could you perhaps "trim the fat" from this collection by getting rid of duplicates or getting rid of the items you no longer use? Also, could you perhaps cut down on your spending on that hobby? Focus on trimming the things you don't feel strongly about – if you dig into things that *bother* you, you're going to eventually relapse.

4. Sign up for every free customer rewards program you can. Even if you rarely shop at that place, having a rewards card for that place will eventually net you some coupons and discounts. Here's the basic game plan for maximizing these programs: create a Gmail address just for these mailings, collect every card you can, and then check that account for extra coupons whenever you're ready to shop.

5. Make your own gifts instead of buying stuff from the store. You can make food mixes, candles, bread, cookies, soap, and all kinds of other things at home quite easily and inexpensively. These make spectacular gifts for others because they involve your homemade touch, plus quite often they're consumable, meaning they don't wind up filling someone's closet with junk. Even better – include a personal handwritten note with the gift. This will make it even more special than anything you could possibly buy down at the mall, plus it saves you money.

6. Master the thirty day rule. Whenever you're considering making an unnecessary purchase, wait thirty days and then ask yourself if you still want that item. Quite often, you'll find that the urge to buy has passed and you'll have saved yourself some money by simply waiting. If you want, you can even keep a "thirty day list" where you write down the item and the day you'll reconsider it, but I prefer just to keep this one in my head – that way, I often just forget about the unimportant things.

7. Write a list before you go shopping – and stick to it. One should *never* go into a store without a strong idea of what one will be buying while in there. Make a careful plan of what you'll buy before you go, then stick strictly to that list when you go to the store. Don't put anything in the cart that's not on the list, no matter how tempting, and you'll come out of the store saving a bundle.

8. Invite friends over instead of going out. Almost every activity at home is less expensive than going out. Invite some friends over and have a cookout or a potluck meal, then play some cards and have a few drinks. Everyone will have fun, the cost will be low, and the others will likely reciprocate not long afterwards.

9. Instead of throwing out some damaged clothing, repair it instead. Don't toss out a shirt because of a broken button – sew a new one on with some closely-matched thread. Don't toss out pants because of a hole in them – put in a patch of some sort and save them for times when you're working around the house. Simple sewing can be done by anyone – it just takes a few minutes and it saves a lot of money by keeping you from buying new clothes when you don't really need to.

10. Don't spend big money entertaining your children. Most children, especially young ones, can be entertained very cheaply. Buy them an end roll of newspaper from your local paper and let their creativity run wild. Make a game out of ordinary stuff around the house, like tossing pennies into a jar, even. Realize that what your children want most of all is your *time*, not your stuff, and you'll find money in your pocket and joy in your heart.

11. Call your credit card company and ask for a rate reduction. Take any of your credit cards that are carrying a balance, flip them over, and call the number on the back. Tell them that you want an interest rate reduction or you'll take your business elsewhere. If the first person you talk to won't do it, ask to talk to a supervisor. If you have a $5,000 balance, even a 3% rate reduction saves you $150 a year.

12. Clean out your closet. Go through your closets and try to get rid of some of the stuff in there. You can have a yard sale with it, take it to a consignment shop, or even donate it for the tax deduction – all of which turn old stuff you don't want to use any more into money in your pocket. Not only that, it's often a psychological load off your mind to clean out your closets.

13. Buy video games that have a lot of replay value – and don't acquire new ones until you've mastered what you have. My video game buying habits have changed quite a bit since my "game of the week" days. Now, I focus on games that can be played over and over and over again, and I focus on mastering the games that I buy. Good targets include puzzle games and long, involved quest games – they maximize the value of your gaming dollar.

14. Drink more water. Not only does drinking plenty of water have great health benefits, water drinking has financial benefits, too. Drink a big glass of water before each meal, and not only will you digest it better, you won't eat as much, saving on the ol' food bill. You'll also find yourself feeling a bit better as you begin to get adequately hydrated (most Americans are perpetually somewhat dehydrated).

15. Cut back on the convenience foods – fast foods, microwave meals, and so on. Instead of eating fast food or just nuking some prepackaged food when you get home, try making some simple and healthy replacements that you can take with you. An hour's worth of preparation one weekend can give you a ton of cheap and handy meals that will end up saving you a *lot* of cash and not eat into your time when you're busy.

16. Give up expensive habits, like cigarettes, alcohol, and drugs. Those habits cause money to flow away from you with nothing in return. Call up your fortitude and work hard to kick the habits and you'll find that money staying in your pocket instead of burning up and floating away.

17. Make a quadruple batch of a casserole. Casseroles are nice, easy dishes to prepare, but on busy nights, it's often still easier to just order some take-out or eat out or just plop a prepackaged meal in the oven. Instead, the next time you make a casserole, make *four* batches of it and put the other three in the freezer. Then, the next time you need a quick meal for the family, grab one of those batches and just heat it up – easy as can be. Even better, doing this allows you to buy the ingredients in bulk, making each casserole cheaper than it would be ordinarily – and far, far cheaper than eating out or trying a prepackaged meal.

18. Be diligent about turning off lights before you leave. If you spend one minute turning off lights before a two hour trip, that's the equivalent of earning $50 an hour. That's some impressive savings, particularly if you do it before longer trips. The key is to *use less energy*, particularly when you're not using the device.

19. Swap books, music, and DVDs cheaply on the internet via services like PaperBackSwap. You can very easily swap the books and CDs and DVDs you've grown bored with via the internet with others. Just use sites like PaperBackSwap, clean out your media collection, and trade them with others online. The best part? You'll get a flood of new books (or CDs or DVDs) to enjoy, mailed right to you – for free.

20. Maximize yard sales. I like to stop by yard sales if I see them, but I recognize that often the stuff there is junk.

Thus, <u>I'm careful about what I buy and I use clever tactics to find it – and lower the prices</u>. That way, I wind up with a really big bargain – or else I can just walk away with the money in my pocket, having been entertained for a bit.

21. Install CFL (or, even better, LED) bulbs wherever it makes sense. These bulbs might cost more initially, but they both have a longer life than normal incandescent bulbs and they both eat far less electricity. CFLs tend to use about 25% of the electricity of an incandescent – LEDs use about 2%. CFLs are cheaper than LEDs right now and produce better light, but not quite as good as incandescent bulbs. My policy? Put LEDs in closets and out of the way places, use CFLs for hall and some room lighting, and use incandescent bulbs (until the other bulbs get better) where you read and do other eye-intensive activities. This will trim a significant amount from your electric bill.

22. Install a programmable thermostat. These devices regulate the temperature in your house automatically according to the schedule that you set. Thus, when you're not home, it allows the heating or cooling to turn off for several hours, saving you on your energy bill. A programmable thermostat can easily cut your energy bill by 10 to 20%.

23. Buy appliances based on reliability, not what's cheapest at the store. It's worth the time to do a bit of research when you buy a new appliance. A reliable, energy efficient washer and dryer might cost you quite a bit now, but if it continually saves you energy and lasts for fifteen years, you'll save *significant* money in the long run. When you need to buy an appliance, research it – start with back issues of Consumer Reports at the library. An hour's worth of research can easily save you hundreds of dollars.

24. Clean your car's air filter. A clean air filter can improve your gas mileage by up to 7%, saving you more than $100 for every 10,000 miles you drive in an average vehicle. Plus, cleaning your air filter is easy to do in just a few minutes – just follow the instructions in your automobile's manual and you're good to go.

25. Hide your credit cards. Take your credit cards and put them in a safe place in your home, *not* in your wallet where it's easy to spend them. If you argue that you need it for "emergencies," just be sure to keep a small amount of cash hidden in your wallet for these emergencies. Don't keep plastic on you until you have the willpower to not use it even when you're sorely tempted.

26. Plan your meals around your grocery store's flyer. Instead of just planning your meals based on a cookbook or whatever you can dream up, plan all your meals around what's on sale in your grocery store's flyer. Look at the biggest sales, then plan meals based on those ingredients and what you have on hand, and you'll find yourself with a much smaller food bill than you're used to.

27. Do a price comparison – and find a cheaper grocery store. Most of us get in a routine of shopping at the same grocery store, even though quite often it's not the one that offers the best deals on our most common purchases. Fortunately, there's a simple way to find the cheapest store around. Just keep track of the twenty or so things you buy most often, then shop for these items at a variety of stores. Eventually, one store will come out on top for your purchases – just make that one your regular shopping destination and you'll automatically save money.

28. Challenge yourself to try making your own things. Before I tried it myself, I thought homemade breadmaking was complicated and a waste of time and money. I came to find out that it was pretty easy and it was actually much cheaper, healthier, and tastier than buying a loaf from the store. Now, we rarely ever buy bread products at the store – and we save money by making that choice.

29. Don't spend money just to de-stress. Quite often, I used to spend money just to wind down from a stressful day at work. Instead, I've found that I quite often feel much better by going home and taking some quiet time just to stretch and then meditate. I end up feeling much more together, happy, and ready to face an evening with the kids in the right mindset than I ever would by just blowing some cash after work. Instead of spending to de-stress, try some basic meditation techniques, stretching, or yoga and see how you feel.

30. Talk to your loved ones about what your dreams are. This seems like an odd way to save money, but think about it. If you spend time with the people you love the most and come to some consensus about your dreams, it becomes easy for you all to plan for it. If you're all planning and working together towards this dream, it becomes easier to stay focused on it and reach it. Set a big, audacious goal together and encourage each other to be financially fit – soon, you'll find you're doing it naturally and your dreams are coming closer than ever.

31. Do a "maintenance run" on your appliances. Check them to make sure there isn't any dust clogging them and that they're fairly clean. Look behind the appliances, and use your vacuum to gently clear away dust. Check all of the vents, especially on refrigerators, dryers, and heating and cooling units. The less dust you have blocking the mechanics of these devices, the more efficiently they'll run (saving you on your energy bill) and the longer they'll last (saving you on replacement costs).

32. Cancel unused club memberships. Are you paying dues at a club that you never use? Like, for instance, a gym membership or a country club membership? Cancel these club memberships, even if you think you *might* use them again someday – you can always renew the membership at a later date if it turns out that you actually do miss it.

33. When shopping for standard items (clothes, sports equipment, older games, etc.), start by shopping used. Quite often, you can find the exact item you want with a bit of clever shopping at used equipment stores, used game stores, consignment shops, and so on. Just make these shops a part of your normal routine – go there first when looking for potential items and you *will* save money.

34. Keep your hands clean. This one's simple – just wash your hands thoroughly each time you use the bathroom or handle raw foods. You'll keep yourself from acquiring all kinds of viruses and bacteria, saving you on medical bills and medicine costs and lost productivity. That's not to say you shouldn't explore the world and get your hands dirty sometimes – that's good for you, too – but basic sanitation does help keep the medical bills away.

35. Remove your credit card numbers from your online accounts. It's easy to spend online when you have your card information stored in an account – just click and buy. The best way to break this habit is to simply delete your card from the account. That way, when you're tempted to spend, you'll be forced to spend the time to dig out your card – and really think about why you're spending this money.

36. Give a gift of a service instead of an item. For new parents, give an evening of babysitting as a gift. If you know pet owners, offer to take care of their pets when they travel. Offer up some lawn care as a gift to a new homeowner. These are always spectacular gifts for anyone – I know that, as a parent of a toddler and an infant, I *love* receiving a babysitting gift, probably more than any "stuff" I might receive.

37. Do holiday shopping right after the holidays. Most people use this technique for Christmas, but it works for every holiday. Wait until about two days after a holiday, then go out shopping for items you need that are themed for that day. Get a Mother's Day card for next year the day after Mother's Day. Get Easter egg decorating kits the day after Easter. Get wrapping paper and cards and such the day after Christmas. The discounts are tremendous, and you can just put this stuff in the closet until next year, saving you a bundle.

38. Join up with a volunteer program. It's a great way to meet new people, get some exercise, and involve yourself in a positive project that can lift your spirit. It also comes without a cost to you and can provide a lot of entertainment and a fulfilling day when you're in the right mindset. I've come to spend more and more of my time volunteering, serving on various committees and groups in the community – and it's the best thing I've ever done.

39. Reevaluate the stuff in the rooms in your house. Go into a room and go through every single item in it. Do you really need that item? Are you happy that it's there, or would you be just fine if it were not? If you can find stuff to get rid of, get rid of it – it just creates clutter and it might have some value to others. You also improve the perceived value of your house – and you're likely to get a lot of cleaning done in the process. It's a frugal win-win-win.

40. Try generic brands of items you buy regularly. Instead of just picking up the ordinary brand of an item you buy, try out the store brand or generic version of the item. Likely, you'll save a few cents now, but you'll also likely discover that the store brand is just as good as the name brand – the only difference between the two, often, is the marketing. Once you're on board the generic train, you'll find your regular grocery bill getting smaller and smaller.

41. Prepare some meals at home. Get an accessible and easy-to-use cookbook (my favorite "beginner" cookbook is Mark Bittman's excellent _How to Cook Everything_) and try making some of the dishes inside. You'll find that cooking at home is much easier than you think – and _way_ cheaper and healthier than take-out or dining out. Even better, you can easily prepare meals in advance – even handy fast food type meals.

42. Switch to term life insurance. Repeat after me: _insurance is not an investment_. Switch to term insurance instead and use that difference in cost to get yourself out of debt and start building some wealth. Universal and whole policies are much more expensive and offer a sub par investment opportunity – you're much better off getting yourself free of a debt burden than spending extra on such things.

43. Go for reliability and fuel efficiency when buying a car. A reliable and fuel efficient car will save you thousands over the long haul. Let's say you drive a vehicle for 80,000 miles. If you choose a 25 miles per gallon car over a 15 miles per gallon car, you save _2,133_ gallons of gas. At $3 a gallon, that's $6,400 in savings right there. Reliability can pay the same dividends. Do the research – it will pay off for you.

44. Don't go to stores or shopping centers for entertainment. Doing so is just an encouragement to spend money you don't really have on stuff you don't really need. Instead, find other places to entertain yourself – the park, the basketball court, a museum, a friend's house, or even in your own home. Don't substitute shopping for entertainment and you'll be way better off.

45. Master the ten second rule. Whenever you pick up an item in order to add it to your cart or to take it to the checkout, stop for ten seconds and ask yourself *why* you're buying it and whether you actually *need* it or not. If you can't find a good answer, put the item back. This keeps me from making impulse buys on a regular basis.

46. Rent out unused space in your home. Do you have an extra bedroom that's not being used? Rent it out. In our home, we could, if times were tough, rent out our entire basement – it has a "living room," a bedroom, and a bathroom and has a stairwell right by the kitchen. If we found the right person, this would bring in a *lot* of extra money.

47. Create a visual reminder of your debt. Basically, just make a giant progress bar that starts with the amount of debt you have and ends with zero. Each time you pay down a little bit, fill in a little more of that progress bar. Keep this reminder in a place where you'll see it often, and keep filling it in regularly. It keeps your eyes on the prize and leads you straight to debt freedom.

48. Get rid of unread magazine subscriptions. Do you have a pile of unread magazines sitting around your house? Likely, it's the result of a subscription that you're not reading. Not only should you not renew that magazine, you should give their subscription department a call and try to cancel for a refund – sometimes, they'll give you the prorated amount back. I've had to cull my subscriptions in the past, but I've never regretted it.

49. Eat breakfast. Eating a healthy breakfast fills you up with energy for the day and also decreases your desire to eat a big lunch in the middle of the day. Not only that, breakfast can be very healthy, quick, and inexpensive. A bowl of oatmeal in the morning is often the one thing that keeps me from running out to eat an expensive lunch later in the day – and it keeps me peppy and full of energy for the entire morning instead of in a coffee-laced daze.

50. Swap babysitting with neighbors. We live in a neighborhood with an army of young children out and about. Because of that, there are a lot of parents out there who are quite willing to swap babysitting nights with us, saving you the money of hiring one for an evening out. A few families even take this to incredible extremes. Try to find another set of parents or two that you trust, and swap nights of babysitting with them. That way, you'll get occasional evenings free without the cost of a babysitter, saving you some scratch.

51. Don't fear leftovers – instead, jazz them up. Many people dread eating leftovers – they're just inferior rehashes of regular meals, not exactly enjoyable to the discerning palate. However, there's nothing cheaper than eating leftovers and with a few great techniques for making leftovers tasty, you can often end up with something surprising and quite delicious on the other end. My favorite technique? *Chaining* – using the leftovers as a basis for an all-new dish.

52. Go through your clothes – all of them. If you have a regular urge to buy clothes, go through *everything* that you have and see what you might find. Take the clothes at the back of the closet and bring them to the front and suddenly your wardrobe will feel completely different. Take the clothes buried in your dresser and pull them to the top. You'll feel like a brand new person who doesn't need to spend money on clothes right now.

53. Brown bag your lunch. Instead of going out to eat at work, take your own lunch. Lots of people think that this means "nasty lunch," but it doesn't. With some thoughtful preparation and just a few minutes of time, you can create something quite enjoyable for your brown bag lunch – and save a fistful of cash each day, too.

54. Learn how to dress minimally. Buy clothes that mix and match well and you'll not need nearly as many clothes. If you have five pants, seven shirts, and seven ties that all go together, you have almost an endless wardrobe right there just by mixing and matching. This is exactly what I do in order to minimize clothes buying and still look professional – I just mix and remix what I wear by using utilitarian clothes options to begin with.

55. Ask for help and encouragement from your inner circle. Sit down and talk to the people you love and care about the most and ask them for help. Tell them that you're trying to trim your spending and you'd love it if they offered any suggestions and support they might have – and *pay attention* to what they tell you. They might have some personal insights for your situation that will really help.

56. If something's broken, give a fair shot at repairing it yourself before replacing it or calling a repairman. Get a handyman's book or advice from the internet and give it a shot yourself. I've fixed clocks, air conditioners, and VCRs by doing this before, saving significant cash by saving on a replacement or on a repair person.

57. Keep <u>an idea notebook in your pocket</u>. I've wasted countless amounts of time and money simply because I've forgotten things in my head. Instead of relying on my memory, I keep a small notebook with me <u>to jot down ideas</u> and things I need to remember, then I check it regularly throughout the day. This keeps me from forgetting to pick up milk and having to backtrack ten miles, for starters.

58. Invest in a deep freezer. A deep freezer, after the initial investment, <u>is a great bargain</u>. You can use it to store all sorts of bulk foods, which enables you to pay less per pound of it at the market. Even better, you can store lots of meals prepared in advance, enabling you to just go home and pop something homemade (and cheap) in the oven.

59. Look for a cheaper place to live. The cost of living in Iowa is <u>surprisingly low</u>, enough so that I'm quite happy to give up the cultural opportunities of other places to enjoy Iowa all year around. When I want to enjoy the cultural opportunities of another place, I'll travel there – after all, I can afford it. Take a serious look about moving to a less expensive area – if you can find work there, then a move can definitely put you in better financial shape.

60. Check out what your town's parks and recreation board has to offer. My town has several wonderful parks, free basketball and tennis courts, free disc golf, trails, and lots of other stuff just there waiting to be used. You can go have fun for hours out in the wonderful outdoors, playing sports, hiking on trails, or trying other activities – and it's all there for free. All you have to do is discover it.

61. Air up your tires. For every two PSI that all of your tires are below the recommended level, you lose 1% on your gas mileage. Most car tires are five to ten PSI below the normal level, so that means by just airing up your tires, you can improve your gas mileage by up to 5%. It's easy, too. Just read your car's manual to see what the recommended tire pressure is, then head to the gas station. Ask the attendant inside if they have a tire air gauge you can borrow (most of them do, both in urban and rural settings), then stop over by the air pump. Check your tires, then use the pump to fill them up to where they should be. It's basically free gas!

62. Start a garden. Gardening is an inexpensive hobby if you have a yard. Just rent a tiller, till up a patch, plant some plants, keep it weeded, and you'll have a very inexpensive hobby that produces a huge amount of vegetables for you to eat at the end of the season. I like planting a bunch of tomato plants, keeping them cared for, then enjoying a huge flood of tomatoes at the end of the summer. We like to eat them fresh, can them, and make tomato juice, sauce, paste, ketchup, pasta sauce, and pizza sauce. Delicious (and very inexpensive)!

63. Dig into your community calendar. There are often tons of free events going on in your town that you don't even know about. Stop by the local library or by city hall and ask how you can get ahold of a listing of upcoming community events, and make an effort to hit the interesting ones. You can often get free meals, free entertainment, and free stuff just by paying attention – even better, you'll get in touch with what's going on around you.

64. Take public transportation. If the city's transit system is available near you, take it to work (or to play) instead of driving your car. It's far cheaper and you don't have to worry about parking your vehicle. When I lived in a larger city, I bought an annual transit pass that actually paid for itself after less than two months of use compared to using an automobile – and after that, for ten months, I basically could ride to work (and to some events) for free. *That's* money in the bank.

65. Cut your own hair. I can cut mine myself with a pair of clippers, for example. I just cut it really short every once in a while and don't worry about it too much. Just put a garbage bag over the bathroom sink, bust out the clippers and scissors, and get it done. Two or three cuts will pay for the clippers, and then you're basically getting free haircuts. With a bit of practice, you can make it look *good*, too.

66. Carpool. Is there anyone that lives near you who works at the same place (or near the same place) that you do? Why not ride together, alternating drivers each day? You can halve the wear and tear and gas costs for your car – and for your acquaintance as well.

67. Design your "debt snowball." Everyone needs a plan to help them get out of debt, so sit down and plot out what debts you're going to pay off and in what order. Simply having a plan goes a long way towards bringing that plan into action, and paying off debts early is one of the surest ways to put money in your pocket over the long run.

68. Get a crock pot. A crock pot is perhaps the best deal on earth for reducing cooking costs in a busy family. You can just dump in your ingredients before work, put it on simmer, and *dinner is*

done when you get home. There are countless recipes out there for all variety of foods, and every time you cook this way, you're saving money as compared to eating out.

69. Do some <u>basic home and auto maintenance on a regular schedule</u>. Instead of just waiting until something breaks to deal with it, develop a monthly maintenance schedule where you go around your home (and your car) and perform a bit of maintenance where it's needed. This little activity, taking you just an hour or two a month, will keep things from breaking down and help you see problems before they become disasters.

70. Pack food before you go on a road trip. Have everyone pack a sack lunch for the trip. That way, instead of stopping in the middle of the trip, driving around looking for a place to eat, spending a bunch of time there, and then paying a hefty bill, you can just eat on the road or, better yet, stop at a nice park and stretch for a bit. Plus, you'll save a lot of money and a fair amount of time this way.

71. Go through your cell phone bill, look for services you don't use, and ditch them. Sit down and go through each item on your bill and see if there's anything there that you don't use, like a surfeit of text messages or web access or something to that effect. Then call your cell phone company and ask to have those services eliminated. Boom, you're saving money.

72. Consolidate your student loans. Interest rates are quite low right now, so it might be worthwhile to consolidate your student loans into one low-rate package. Look into the various student loan consolidation packages – even a 1% reduction on a $10,000 loan saves you $100 a year – and your loan is probably bigger than that (and the rate cut you could get is probably bigger).

73. When buying a car, go for late model used. These are typically cars coming straight off of leases, meaning they were cared for by reliable owners. My truck was purchased with this criteria and has lasted me several years already with only one significant issue – and I saved a ton of money on the purchase price over buying new. Only now is it beginning to show significant signs of aging – and with the money I saved on that purchase, I was able to get out of debt that much quicker.

74. Hit the library – *hard*. Don't look at a library as just a place to get old books. Look at it as a free place to do all sorts of things. I've used it to learn a foreign language, meet people, use the Internet anonymously, check out movies and CDs, grab local free newspapers, and keep up on community events. Best of all, it doesn't cost a dime.

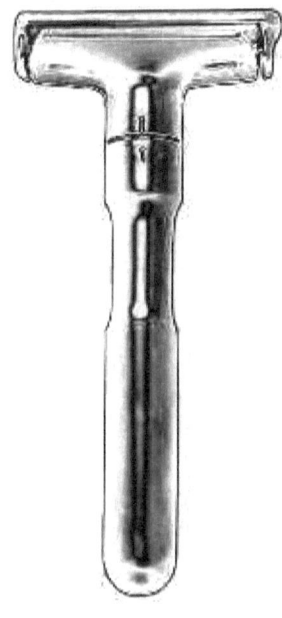

75. Use a simple razor to shave. I've been a big advocate of the basic safety razor for a long time, but that's just one piece of the puzzle. For "normal" shaves, I just shave in the shower and dry off the blade afterwards, using just soap for lather – incredibly cheap, since I only swap blades once every few weeks. The real moral of the story? Use a simple razor – not an expensive electric one that stops working in three years – and shave your face when it's wet. You can get a very good shave with some practice and save a lot of money over the long haul.

76. Find daily inspiration for making intelligent moves.
I'm usually inspired by my children. Perhaps you're inspired to make changes by your spouse – or even by someone in the community you respect. Maybe it's just a personal goal, like an early retirement. Find something that makes you *want* to make positive changes, then use that person or thing as a constant reminder. Keep a picture of it in your wallet, in your vehicle, and on your bathroom mirror. Keep it in your mind as much as you possibly can.

77. Find out about *all* of the benefits of your job. Most people aren't even aware of all of the benefits available to them. Spend some time with an HR person finding out about *all* the benefits of your job – you might be surprised at what you might find. I found free tickets to sporting events, free personal improvement opportunities, and an optional employee match on some retirement funds that maximized the money I was socking away. This not only cut down on my own spending on things like sporting and community events and educational classes, but also improved my retirement plan.

78. Make your own items instead of buying them. I like to make my own laundry detergent and my own Goo-Gone, for starters. I also like making Glade, Windex, and Soft Scrub. In both cases, it's way cheaper than buying the commercial version. Hunt around for recipes – it's amazing how many things you can make at home in just a few minutes that saves a ton of money compared to the commercial version.

79. Encourage your friends to do less expensive activities. This is often a tricky thing to do, but there are a number of techniques you can try. My favorite one is to be the first one to suggest something – that often gives you the power to steer the group towards things that are cheaper. If you can convince your friends to go to the park and shoot hoops instead of going golfing, those green fees are going to stay in your pocket.

80. Don't speed. Not only is it inefficient in terms of gasoline usage, it also can get you pulled over and cost you a bundle, as I discovered a while back. It's highly cost-efficient to just drive the speed limit, keep that gas in the tank, and keep the cops off your tail.

81. Read more. Reading is one of the cheapest – and most beneficial – hobbies around. Most towns have a library available to the public – just go there and check out some books that interest you. Then, spend some of your free time in a cozy place in your house, just reading away. You'll learn something new, improve your reading ability, enjoy yourself, and not have to spend a dime. Here are some more techniques for getting into the reading flow.

82. Buy a smaller house. I currently live in a 2,000 square foot house with my wife and two kids. Frankly, it's just the right size for us – if anything, it's a little big. We often find ourselves in the same room in the house, just surrounded by empty space. You don't need a giant place to live. Instead, buy something more modest and you'll find yourself with plenty of room – and still plenty of cash in your pocket.

83. Drive a different route to work. This is an especially powerful tip if you find yourself "automatically" stopping for something on the way into work or the way home. Get rid of that constant drain by selecting a different route that doesn't go by the temptation, even if the new route is a bit longer. You'll still be time ahead (because you're not stopping) and you'll definitely be money ahead.

84. *Always* ask for fees to be waived. Any time you sign up for a service of any kind and there are sign-up fees, ask for them to be waived. Sometimes (but not always), they will be – and you save money just by being forthright about not wanting to pay excessive fees. I did this with my last cell phone sign-up and got part of my fees waived, cutting down significantly on the bill.

85. Don't overspend on hygiene products. For most people, inexpensive hygiene products do the trick – for example, I just buy whichever toothpaste is the cheapest, and the same goes with deodorant and the like. The key is to use this stuff regularly and consistently – bathe daily, keep yourself clean, and you'll be just fine. No need to buy a $40 facial scrub if you actually scrub your face properly.

86. Eat less meat. For the nutritional value, meat is very expensive, especially as compared to vegetables and fruits. Simply change around your regular meal proportions to include more fruits and vegetables and less meats – eat a smaller steak and a bigger helping of green beans, for example. Not only is this a healthier way to eat (saving on health costs), it's also less expensive.

87. Use a brutally effective coupon strategy. Here's the trick: wait a month before using the coupons. Save your coupon flyer out of your Sunday paper for a month, then bust it out and start cutting anything that might be of interest. For a bonus kicker, use the coupons in comparison with your grocery store flyer that week to find out ways you can use a coupon to reduce the cost of an item already on sale – you can wind up paying pennies for some things and, on occasion, actually get food for free (I've came home with a ton of free yogurt containers before, for example).

88. Air seal your home. Most homes have some air leaks that make the job of keeping it cool in summer and warm in winter that much harder – and that much more costly for you. Spend an afternoon air sealing your home – the DoE has a great guide on basic airsealing.

89. Make your own beer or wine. If you enjoy an occasional drink, this is a great way to enjoy some of the beverages that you love at a very cheap price. You can easily make five gallons of beer or wine at once and it doesn't take that long, either, once you have the basic ingredients. Even better, it's a great activity to do with friends – you buy the equipment, they bring the juice and you both get a few bottles of delicious homemade wine out of the deal. A nice entertainment, plus some free beverages – that's a great frugal deal.

90. Make sure all your electrical devices are on a surge protector. This is especially true of your entertainment center and your computer equipment. A power surge can damage these electronics very easily, so spend the money for a basic surge protector and keep your equipment plugged into such a device.

91. Get on an automatic debt repayment plan for any student loans you have. Many student loans offer a rate reduction if you sign up for their automatic debt repayment plan. This way, not only do you save a few bucks a month, you don't have to go to the effort of actually paying the bill. Our automatic plan saved us about $60 a year.

92. Cut down on your vacation spending. Instead of going on a big, extravagant trip, pack up the car and see some of America some years for vacation. One of the best vacations I've ever taken was when my son was an infant – we just packed up the car and drove around Minnesota, eventually camping for a few days along the north shore of Lake Superior. For a week long relaxing vacation, it was incredibly cheap and quite memorable, too.

93. Cancel the cable or satellite channels you don't watch. Many people with cable services often are paying for a premium package but rarely watch those extra channels. For the longest time, my wife and I were subscribed to HBO, Starz, and Cinemax, yet we would only tune in once a month at best. We argued that it was worth it because we could watch a movie or a great drama whenever we wanted, but it would have been far cheaper just to rent a movie. Get rid of the excess channels and put that cash back in your pocket.

94. Exercise more. Go for a walk or a jog each evening, and practice stretching and some light muscle exercise at home. These exercises can be done at home for very little, meaning you've got an activity without a lot of cost, and the health benefits are enormous. Just set aside some time each day to get some exercise, and your body *and wallet* will thank you.

95. Utilize online bill pay with your bank. This serves two purposes. First, it keeps you in much closer contact with your money, as you can keep a very close eye on your balance and be in much less danger of overdrafting. Second, it saves you money on stamps and paper checks by allowing you to just fill in an online form, click submit, and have your bill paid. Try it out – and take advantage of it if you're not already.

96. Buy staples in bulk. We buy items we use a lot of in bulk, particularly items that don't perish – trash bags, laundry detergent, diapers, and so on are purchased in the largest amounts possible. This cuts down on their cost per usage by quite a bit and, over the long haul, begins to add up to some serious money. Even better, we don't have to shop for these items very often, saving time and a fraction of the cost of a trip to the grocery store.

97. Connect your entertainment center and/or computer setup to a true smart power strip. A device like the SmartStrip LCG4 basically cuts power to all devices on the strip depending on the status of the first item on the strip. So, if you have your workstation hooked up to this, every time you power down your workstation, your monitor powers down, your printer powers down, your scanner powers down, and so on. You can do the same thing with your entertainment console – when you turn off the television, the cable/satellite box also goes off, as does the video game console, the VCR, the DVD player, and so on. This can save you a *lot* of electricity and significantly trim your power bill.

98. Don't beat yourself up when you make a mistake. Even if you make ten good choices, it's easy to beat yourself up and feel like a failure over one bad choice. If you make a big mistake and *realize it*, think about why you realized it now instead of then, and try to apply that later on. The memory of that mistake can end up being very valuable, indeed.

99. Always keep looking ahead. Don't let the mistakes of your past drag you down into more mistakes. Look ahead to the future. The choices you make now won't affect the past – but they definitely will affect the future. Think back, and remember how the bad choices you made earlier are costing you now, and constantly remember to not make those mistakes now so that they don't cost your future self.

100. Never give up. Whenever the struggle against debt feels like it's too much, go read a personal finance blog and remember that there are a lot of people out there fighting the same fight. Read around through the archives and learn some new things – and perhaps get inspired to keep going, no matter what.

PS:

In this book, you have learned one of the ways we save money. For my family and me it is a very powerful method. While we have saved quite a bit of money it is nothing compared to the amount of money we have made investing in ourselves and learning how to help others.

We invite you to visit my website to learn more, but before you do take a listen to this short recording (212) 461-2954. It can't harm you, it may just help you and if you decide to learn more about investing in yourself, it may just change your life.

I thank you for getting my book and I know that you will be blessed as soon as you start getting your coupons and start saving. I know that this book is short but how hard is it to give people what they want and need, when you take out all of the junk you're left with the important stuff.

To Your Success,

Maxwell Toliver,

http://www.maxwelltoliver.net

maxwelltoliver@gmail.com

www.ingramcontent.com/pod-product-compliance
Lightning Source LLC
Chambersburg PA
CBHW031253280526
45784CB00004B/1841